Mik

The Inspirational Story of Baseball Superstar Mike Trout

Table of Contents

Introduction

As the title implies, this is a short book about [The Inspirational Story of Baseball Superstar Mike Trout] and how he rose from his life in New Jersey to become one of today's leading and most respected baseball players. In his rise to superstardom, Mike has inspired not only the youth, but fans of all ages throughout the world.

This book also portrays the crucial moments that Mike had to go through during his early childhood and teen years until he became who he is today. A great source of inspiration is Mike's service to the community and his strong connection with the fans of his sport. He continues to serve as the jovial stud, who loves to play the superstar role and prove doubters wrong every game.

Combining incredible strength, lightning quick speed, a strong throwing arm, and superior coordination, Mike has demonstrated the ability to change the outcome of any game. From being a phenomenal man-child to becoming one of the greatest young ball players of his generation, you'll learn how this man has risen to the ranks of the best baseball players today.

Thanks again for grabbing this book. Hopefully you can take some of the lessons and examples from Mike's story and apply them to your own life!

Chapter 1:

The Early Days of the Millville Meteor

The first time you watch Mike "The Millville Meteor" Trout hit a ball or play defense in the outfield, you'll see a man who is seemingly made to play the game of baseball at a high level. However, of course, even the most elite of performers have a back story that helped them get to where they are now.

Michael Nelson Trout was born on August 7th, 1991 in Millville, New Jersey. His parents are Jeff and Debbie Trout. They were a middle-class family and Mike's parents allowed him to become engaged in all kinds of activities from an early age.

The biggest influence on Mike to play baseball was his father, Jeff. Jeff was an accomplished high school baseball player at Millville. Later, he took his talents to the University of Delaware and then went on to get picked in the fifth round of the 1982 MLB Draft by the Minnesota Twins. And while he had shown promise as a baseball player, a knee injury signaled the end of his baseball career in 1986.

From a young age, it was apparent that Mike got some of his natural baseball talents from his father. He also displayed some incredible characteristics that go beyond the game of baseball. More than just having an elite-level athletic ability as a child, Mike was regarded as mentally advanced for his age.

He had an incredible amount of patience as a child; he was able to sit through an entire baseball game at the age of 8. What's more, it was very apparent that, compared to his peers, his maturity regarding baseball strategy and attitude, was much more advanced.

It was quickly obvious that he possessed something special, becoming a force in Little League. Mike Kavanagh, his former coach in Little League and the Ripken League, says that young Mike was dominating leagues played by 12 year olds at the age of 9.

He was dominating those games with a combination of size (a trait he shared with his dad), his skills (his 2-way skills allowed him to play multiple positions well), and his instincts (this was always one thing that has made him stand out on the field).

Of course, these signals were just the beginning, as this legend continued to grow with each passing year.

High School Phase

Mike went on to play high school baseball in his hometown. He enrolled at Millville Senior High, the same school where he first got engaged in the game, by shagging fly balls and being the varsity squad's bat boy. When he entered high school, Mike played two different positions and played each of them quite well. As a pitcher, he had the reputation of throwing some mean fastballs.

He also played shortstop, the same position that his childhood hero, Derek Jeter, played. In fact, Jeter was the reason Mike wore number 2 early in his career (he later made the switch to number 1). Mike made a position switch from shortstop to centerfield, where he still retained his incredible instincts on the defensive side of the ball.

Unlike some child phenoms, Mike did not immediately play baseball nor spend his entire time in high school solely playing this game. He was also a distinguished basketball player. Mike earned five letters between baseball and basketball throughout his time in high school. Specifically, he garnered three letters in baseball and two letters in basketball.

By the time that he was a sophomore, Mike was already making headlines as a legit baseball prospect. He displayed dead-eye pitching skills, powerful batting force and accuracy, incredible speed (he is capable of getting from home plate to first base in under 4 seconds, an astonishing feat for a right-handed player), and the ability to raise his level of play in big games.

Mike played for coach Roy Hallenbeck during his sophomore year of high school. One of his best games was when he played on the mound in a game against the Vineland Fighting Clan, the Thunderbolts' biggest rival, which the school was not able to defeat since 2003. Mike led the team consisting of 9 seniors to a 2-1 win by firing a complete game two-hitter.

Mike's junior year was a great starting point for his baseball career. One of the highlights was when his team played against the Egg Harbor Township High School. In this particular game, he threw a no-hitter and fanned 18 batters. This greatly helped his team win and eventually make it to the state playoffs.

There, they were defeated by the Cougars from Cherry Hill High School East. In this game, Mike was intentionally walked by the Cougars. This included an instance when all the bases were loaded, and then once when he represented one run that had potential for a victory.

In his senior year, Mike was later shifted to the outfield from his initial position at shortstop and pitcher. It was also during this year that he hit 18 home runs, an outstanding record for a New Jersey high school baseball player.

By the age of 14, Mike was already working with coaches at the Tri-State Arsenal. He played travel ball with this program, which is among the northeast's premier travel programs. He was able to play in a number of different tournaments under this program, which included the Perfect Game WWBA Championships held in 2007 and 2008, both in Jupiter, Florida.

During the summer before Mike's senior year of high school, he went to Southern California to attend the Area Code Games. Here, Mike went against some of the country's best players, 6-for-11, and this caught the attention of an Angels scout named Greg Morhardt.

Incidentally, Morhardt played with Mike's dad in the Minor Leagues during his time. Morhardt claimed Mike Trout was the strongest and the fastest 17-year-old baseball player he had ever seen.

Of course, there were initial worries, such as the fact that New Jersey had not been producing quality high school prospects. This could mean the level of competition that Mike was playing against could be sub-par compared to other prospects around the country, thus inflating his numbers.

However, Morhardt and the Angels were sold on his talent and were dead-set to pick Mike using the 25th pick in the 2009 MLB Draft.

To the relief of the Angels, Mike fell all the way to them at the 25th pick, despite intense interest from their rival team, the Oakland Athletics, on draft day. Upon getting drafted, Mike immediately signed with the Angels.

Armed with a $1.2 million dollar signing bonus, he immediately went to work in the Arizona

Rookie League. It was in the Minor Leagues where Mike's potential stood out even further.

Chapter 2:

The Growth of a Prospect

Not surprisingly, the Los Angeles Angels felt extremely relieved that their top prospect, Mike Trout, was able to slip down the draft. Almost immediately, that relief turned into a feeling of being lucky and blessed, as Mike proved to the Angels that they made the right choice.

In his very first game in the Minor Leagues, Mike reached base six times, an astounding number for any level of competitive baseball. Showing dead-eye accuracy and incredible speed, Mike hit .360 in his first year, while giving infielders headaches when trying to throw him out. He was simply dominating the competition.

Making A Splash

Mike's first year statistics included hitting .360 with .506 SLG and a .418 OBP, with 1 home run. He had 25 RBI. He also recorded 13 stolen bases in his 187 plate appearances.

His rookie season was not spent entirely with the Angels, however. He also played for another team, the Cedar Rapids Kernels, which was part of Class A Midwest League. Shortly after his eighteenth birthday, Mike was promoted to the Cedar Rapids Kernels.

During the five games in which he appeared, Mike listed hitting numbers of .267/.421/.267 in 20 plate appearances. By the end of the year, he was already rated as the third-best prospect in the Angels pipeline. In his second season playing for the Kernels, Mike was able to post some incredible statistics in the 82 games that he played.

Registering .362/.454/.526 hitting percentages, he also recorded six home runs, 45 stolen bases, and 39 runs batted in. By the end of the year, Mike was named the Topps Minor League Player of the Year for 2010, the youngest ever to do so (19 years, 2 months).

He also received recognition as a Topps Class A All-Star, as well as *Baseball America* All-Star status. Moreover, he was rated as the second-best baseball prospect for that year.

It was also during this time when *Baseball America* rated Mike 85th best in the entire baseball world. Shortly afterwards, he was selected to take part in the All-Star Futures Games. He was promoted after the All-Star Futures Games to the Rancho Cucamonga Quakes, which belonged to the Class A Advanced California League.

By the year 2011, all of the organizations around the MLB were paying close attention to the play of Mike Trout. In most of the 2011 preseason listings, including ESPN and the MLB Network, he was listed as the best Minor League prospect in the entire league, regardless of position.

That season, he played with the AA League team Arkansas Travelers, where he would play 91 games and post .326/.414/.544 hitting averages, 11 home runs, 38 RBI, 82 runs scored and 33 stolen   bases.

2011 - Playing for the Los Angeles Angels of Anaheim

On July 8th, 2011, Mike was promoted to the Los Angeles Angels of Anaheim. He replaced centerfielder Peter Bourios, who was injured. That night, Mike made his debut in the Major Leagues and went 0-for-3.

He recorded his first career hit in his next game. This was an infield single played at the bottom of the third inning against Michael Pineda, the pitcher of the Seattle Mariners.

Mike's first MLB home run came during the July 24th game against the Baltimore Orioles, pitched by Mark Worrell. On August 1st, 2011, Mike returned to Double A Arkansas, after he hit .163, which included 1 home run and 6 RBI in 12 starts while playing for the Angels.

On August 19th, 2011, the Angels recalled Mike. On that night, he went 1-for-4, which included a home run. During the game on August 30th of the same year, he hit 2 home runs, making him the youngest Angels player to accomplish that feat in just one game. He homered off Anthony Vasquez, a pitcher of the Mariners, in the top of the game's second inning and in the top of the fourth inning.

Mike's 2011 season was impressive, earning him various awards, votes, and recognition. After hitting .326/.414/.544, with 38 RBI, 11 home runs, 33 stolen bases, and 82 runs scored in 91 games, Mike garnered the attention as *Baseball America's* Minor League Player of the Year. He was also named an outfielder on the All-Star team of *Baseball America's* 2011 Minor League Team.

While those were very impressive awards, no one could have predicted what Mike Trout would bring to the table during the first full year of his MLB career.

Chapter 3:

The Super Rookie

Aiming to build on his fantastic 2011 season, Mike started the 2012 season for the AAA-League team, the Salt Lake Bees. He played in Tacoma alongside the Salt Lake Bees in the Triple A Pacific Coast League Season.

Mike remembers it vividly as freezing, but the weather did not stop him from making at least one spectacular play game after game.

On opening day, straight from an early flight, Mike punched out 3 singles. He also scored twice. Mike, on a single, scored from first base -

a story that fans love to tell over and over to this day. That was how great he played on that day, despite the weariness from travel and the cold. There wasn't even any sunlight, as the team recalled.

In 20 games with the Bees, Mike posted some incredible statistics, with the most glaring being a .401/.487/.723 hitting line. By the end of the month, he had made it back to the Majors. He debuted on April 28th, and from then on, Mike authored the greatest rookie season in the entire history of baseball.

Meanwhile, the Angels' main slugger, Bobby Abreu, had been struggling at the plate. He was batting .208 in 24 at-bats. On April 28th, the Angels called up Mike to replace Abreu, who had just been traded. Almost immediately, Mike made an impact for the Angels.

It was very apparent that the 2012 Mike Trout was very different from the 2011 Mike Trout.

After getting his bearings in the Majors for a few days, he simply exploded onto the scene in May. During that month, Mike played like a true 2-way beast, hitting home runs, stealing bases, and playing incredible defense as an outfielder. His hitting percentage rose above .350, and he led the league in runs scored and reaching bases for the months of May and June.

More important than the individual accolades, Mike provided a shot in the arm for the Los Angeles Angels. Before he came in, the Angels' record was 6-14 and the team was in danger of falling out of the AL playoff race by the All-Star break.

Mike combined forces with Torii Hunter, Albert Pujols, and Mark Trumbo to lead the team to a 32-18 record in Mike's first 50 games as a pro. By the All-Star break, not only did Mike get to play in the 2012 MLB All-Star Game, but he also opened the discussion regarding who the season's best rookie was.

On June 4th, Mike recorded the first four-hit game of his career. Fifteen days later, he recorded the second one of his career. During this time, he was able to score all 4 times and 2 of his 4 hits were at least doubles.

From June 4th-10th, Mike was named American League Co-Player of the Week, along with Torii Hunter, the Angels' rightfielder. During this period, Mike went 13-for-25, posting a batting average of .520 along with 4 stolen bases and 10 runs scored.

On June 27th, in a game against the Baltimore Orioles, Mike recorded his third career four-hit game. All these he achieved in a single month, catapulting him further into the limelight. In this same game against the Orioles, Mike was able to showcase his defensive skills.

This was highlighted when he robbed a home run from J.J. Hardy, the Orioles' shortstop. He made a spectacular catch by leaping over the center field wall during the bottom of the first inning.

While playing in his first All-Star game against the New York Mets, Mike singled off rival pitcher, R.A. Dickey, in the bottom of the game's 6th inning. He also drew base on balls against Aroldis Chapman, the Cincinnati Reds' pitcher, in the bottom of the 7th inning.

In June, Mike batted .372, with 16 RBI and 3 home runs. He was named the AL Rookie of the Month and AL Player of the Month. His impact on the team's performance did not go unnoticed among management.

According to Mike Scioscia, the Angels' team manager, there are very few players in the game who could come along and do as much as what Mike had done. He further stated that Mike's performance and the results of his talent do not come as a surprise because he was already a very extraordinary talent as a rookie.

By the time July and August rolled around, there was no doubt in anyone's mind that Mike was now the big star in Los Angeles. This was no small feat considering the quality of his teammates, namely Pujols and Hunter. Nonetheless, he became the first American League rookie to win both Rookie of the Month and Player of the Month in the same month, during July.

In August, Mike also became the youngest player to hit 20 home runs and record 40 stolen bases in just 1 season. The previous holder of this record was Cesar Cedeño, former centerfielder of the Houston Astros, who accomplished this feat back in 1972. Mike also became the youngest hitter to achieve at least 30 stolen bases and at least 20 home runs in a single season.

Needless to say, Mike broke a lot of records during this run, matching or eclipsing records set by stars and Hall of Famers, such as Joe DiMaggio, Ichiro Suzuki, and Hal Trosky. The 26 stolen bases tied Mike with Jerry Remy, by the All-Star Break, for the rookie franchise record for the most number of stolen bases.

During the July 22nd game, Mike broke 2 records at once. He broke the American League rookie and the Angels franchise record by crossing home plate after scoring a run in 14 consecutive games. His 34 runs scored for the games in July tied the Major League rookie record held by Hal Trosky, first baseman of the Cleveland Indians, who claimed that record back in 1934.

Mike also posted 10 home runs, 23 RBI, and a .392 batting average during this period. He continued to display his speed during these games as well. He stole 9 bases and scored 32 runs in July games alone. Mike became the first rookie since Joe DiMaggio's 1936 season, when he scored 80 runs and drove in at least 55 runs in 81 games.

In the August 4th game against the Chicago White Sox, Mike yet again made a highlight catch. This catch robbed Gordon Beckham, the White Sox second baseman, of a home run during the second inning. The catch was so spectacular that during an interview after this particular game, White Sox catcher A.J. Pierzynski was quoted to have said that Trout makes outfield catches look so great.

In the August 21st game against the Red Sox, Mike went 2-for-4 in a victory. This game raised his batting average up to .344. With this new average, Mike once again set a rookie record - this time for batting average in 100 games. He finished August with 7 home runs, 11 stolen bases, .866 OPS, 19 RBI, and a .284 batting average.

And with these eye popping numbers, it wasn't very surprising that Mike was hailed once again as Rookie of the Month for August - his fourth time achieving the honor. And by winning this award, Mike became the first American rookie to gain this achievement since 2001, when Ichiro Suzuki won this same award 4 times in a single season.

On August 26th, Mike scored his season's 100th run. This made him the 2nd Angels rookie to garner 100 runs in just 1 season. The first one to set this record was Devon White. Mike went further by surpassing White's record for the number of runs in a season.

On this same day, he set a new Angels record for the number of runs scored in a rookie season. He scored 3 runs in this game, which was the tenth time already in the 2012 season where he had scored at least 3 runs in a game. This was the most since 2001's 11 games by the legendary Sammy Sosa.

By September and October, people began to realize that Mike Trout's early success was not a fluke. He became the first rookie since Ichiro to score more than 120 runs, became the youngest-ever member of the 30-30 club, broke Vladimir Guerrero's record for most runs scored in one season in Angels history, and became the first-ever player to record 30 home runs, steal 45 bases, and score 125 runs, all in a single season.

In a September 9th game against the Detroit Tigers, Mike achieved yet another record. In this game, he made history by becoming the first player under 22 years of age to hit a leadoff home run in back-to-back games. On September 21st, Mike crossed the 120 run mark, surpassing the one set by Ichiro, and becoming the fourth rookie overall to achieve this since 1964.

On the 30th of September, Mike joined the 30-30 club. This made him the youngest player to ever get this distinction. He achieved this when he belted off Yu Darvish's seventh inning pitch to help the Angels win 5-4.

Mike's record-setting and record-breaking streak continued. He surpassed Wally Joyner's record for the most hits in a season, totaling 173. He also set the record as the first rookie to steal 40 bases and hit 30 home runs in a single season.

In the American League, Mike finished second in batting average (.326) and in OPS (.963), first in OPS+ (171), third in OBP (on-base percentage, .399) and slugging percentage (.564), and ninth in hits (182). Mike also became the first Angels player to lead in stolen bases (49), surpassing Chone Figgins' 2005 record.

Mike's impressive rookie year finished with a WAR (wins above replacement) value of 10.9, according to Baseball-Reference.com. He was 2.4 points better than Robinson Cano from the Yankees, who was the year's second place finisher. Mike's WAR value made him the first position player to get an above 10.0 WAR score since the time of Barry Bonds of the San Francisco Giants.

Bonds went for 11.6 WAR score in 2001 and 2002. There were only 3 other players who produced better WAR at ages younger than 25 years old. They were Babe Ruth, who had 11.6 WAR in 1920 at the age of 25, Lou Gehrig with 11.5 WAR in 1927 at the age of 24, and Mickey Mantle with 11.1 WAR at the age of 25 in 1957.

Mike only played 139 games, coming to the Angels after the season had already commenced. But in these games, he was able to lead the team in runs scored, batting average, stolen bases, triples, base on balls, on-base percentage, batting average, hits, total bases, on-base plus slugging, and slugging percentage.

Within the Angels' roster, Mike was tied with Albert Pujols for second place in home runs.

Mark Trumbo led the team in home runs. Mike was fourth on the team in runs batted in.

With such an incredible run, Mike became the unanimous winner of the 2012 AL Rookie of the Year award, sweeping all Rookie of the Month honors along the way. He also won the BBWAA Jackie Robinson Rookie of the Year Award on November 12th, 2012, after he received 28 out of 28 first place votes. He was the 18th rookie to ever win this award unanimously, as well as the first player on the Angels to receive this award since Tim Salmon in 1993.

The rookie awards kept piling up. On November 13th, Mike won the Heart and Hustle Award. This award is given to players who demonstrate an exemplary passion for baseball and who best embody the spirit, tradition, and values of the sport.

Mike also received the Silver Slugger Award, becoming one of 3 outfielders playing in the

American League to receive this award. This was in recognition of their offensive play for their position, which were the best in the majors. The other 2 awardees were the Minnesota Twins' Josh Willingham and the Texas Rangers' Josh Hamilton.

Not only was he considered one of the best rookies in the game, but Mike was also regarded as one of the best players in the game, period. In 2012, he was regarded as a legit challenger for the MVP award, with his chief rival being Detroit Tigers superstar, Miguel Cabrera.

The impact of both Trout and Cabrera, on their respective teams, was more or less unquestioned. They were widely considered the best players on their respective teams and were a huge reason their clubs were competitive for the entire season. The debate mainly circled around the battle of statistics.

Mike was the league leader in the wins above replacement (WAR) rating, with a score of 10.9. Also, he won the 2012 Heart and Hustle Award for exemplifying the passion, values, spirit and tradition of baseball. Lastly, he was awarded the Fielding Bible Award for being MLB's best centerfielder. Not to be outdone, Cabrera also won his share of accolades, including winning the first Triple Crown since 1967 as the AL leader in batting average, home runs, and RBI.

Mike's supporters for his American League MVP bid were banking on his high WAR value. The competition with Cabrera was tagged as a "saber-metrics vs. traditional statistics war". Those supporting and pushing for Trout as MVP were quoting his exemplary WAR. As Jayson Stark wrote about Trout, his 10.5 WAR was "insane" and a clear indication that Trout was the better baseball player, even better than one of baseball's greatest hitters of all time.

If one is to include Mike's slash lines (92.3% stolen base success rate, 62 extra base hits, and other items in his stat sheet), it clearly showed how great a player he was. Stark further wrote that there were no other players in the entire history of the sport who could match Mike's stat sheet slash lines, that combined excellence in several areas, in just 1 season.

On the other side of the debate, Scott Miller of CBS, in siding with Cabrera, wrote that Cabrera was way more than just stats. He wrote that Cabrera combined high stats with "badass lineup" and added great value to his team.

In one of the closest MVP races in recent memory, Cabrera ultimately beat Mike and won the 2012 MVP Award. Still, there was nothing to be taken away from the magical season of Mike Trout. He was seen as perhaps the future of the sport, and at the age of 21, he was definitely not going anywhere.

When later asked about the highly debated MVP bid, Mike was quoted to have been cool with the decision. While fans and supporters may have been very vocal about their disappointment, Mike was not bitter at all. In fact, he was already overwhelmed and appreciative that his name made it into the MVP talks at all, stating that it already gave him a great feeling and was a "pretty cool experience".

Mike's Rookie Year In Review

Rookie Records

The first Major League player to hit better than .320, with 45 stolen bases and 30 home runs in just a single season.

The youngest player in Major League Baseball history to record 25 home runs and 40 stolen bases in a season.

He joined the ranks of the elites, which included:

Ted Williams, Alex Rodriguez, and Mel Ott. Mike joined the group of players that hit .320 or better, with more than 30 home runs during a season in their 20s.

Ty Cobb. Mike was the youngest player (at the age of 21) to post 40 stolen bases in a single season since Cobb's record in 1907.

Hal Trosky, Albert Pujols, Ted Williams, Tony Oliva, and Walt Dropo. Mike joined this group as one of only 6 rookies to hit .320 or above, including more than 30 home runs.

Mike recorded 49 stolen bases out of 53 attempts during his rookie season. This amounted to a percentage of 92.5%. The only other players to have better percentages in this category were Max Carey in 1922 with 96.2% (with 51/53) and Jimmy Rollins in 2008 with 94.0% (47 out of 50).

Mike joined Rickey Henderson to become one of only 2 players in the history of the Major Leagues to hit .350 or above, with 30 or more stolen bases and 15+ home runs (Henderson's average was .352, 47 stolen bases, and 16 home runs, in the 1985 season.).

The Super Rookie Off The Field

It would be easy for a person to become overwhelmed by the amount of attention and recognition that Mike enjoyed in his first full year as a major leaguer.

There are lots of players in all different sports who may have let all the fame and attention to get to their heads, but not Mike. Despite his record-breaking plays and remarkable statistics, he remained a down-to-earth and all-around good guy.

A teammate once said that the fame makes it a little bit harder for Mike to perform simple, everyday tasks like grocery shopping or eating out. It isn't necessarily the paparazzi, but the legions of fans he meets whenever he goes out.

Looking Forward to Sophomore Season

No doubt, Mike Trout was one of baseball's greatest rookies and will most likely turn out to be one of the greatest players of the sport. His statistics in his rookie year made him almost seem too good to be true. With all the records he made and broke, he appeared to be Superman on the field.

He battled a viral infection the previous spring, and he lost around 20 pounds as a result. By the next year, he intentionally gained weight. Some people were apprehensive about his added weight, worrying that his weight might cost him his speed, which was a vital factor in his game.

What they did not realize was that Mike is still in his early 20s and thus still enjoyed high metabolism. In fact, teammates say he can eat 24 chicken wings in under 10 minutes.

Some fans were also concerned about his slight statistical decline during the final two months of his rookie season. Mike appeared human in terms of his .287 average with 67 strikeouts in his last 58 games.

But according to Mike Scioscia, the Angels' team manager, the decline was not an indication of a downgrade in Trout's performance. Mike still played consistently and the statistics may just be a function of the game or that the factors only included a small sample size.

And Mike proved just that in his sophomore season. When asked about falling into that dreaded sophomore slump that plagues a lot of standout rookies, Mike was unconcerned. In fact, he was as confident as ever, despite the issue that the Angels' renewed him for $510,000.

This amount, according to most fans and analysts, was too small in relation to the impact Mike made on the team. He was, nevertheless, unfazed and unconcerned about the amount. He wasn't bitter at all. He was quoted to have said that the numbers do not matter at all. What matters is that he gets the opportunity to go out on the field and play the game he loves.

Fans were actually excited to see what feats he could perform next. He looked well-prepared for his next season. He looked bigger and more excited to play again, despite the issues like his contract and the MVP title, which many fans firmly believed he deserved but didn't get.

This humble demeanor that Mike portrayed, gained him even more fans, as people began to notice how much of a wise professional Mike already was, despite his youthful looks. This personality trait of only focusing on what one can control in any given situation, rather than letting external factors dictate one's mood or performance, is something that we can all take and apply to our own lives.

Chapter 4:

Continued Growth as a Sophomore

For all that he did in his rookie campaign, both critics and fans were expecting more from "King Fish 2.0" in his second season. Fans, both inside and outside Los Angeles, were watching with bated breath to see what Mike Trout had in store.

Mike began the 2013 season in left field, giving up his center field position for the returning Peter Bourjos. However, just like the previous season, Mike started slowly, "only" knocking in 16 RBI and 2 home runs in the month of April.

However, the month did not end without a milestone, as he hit his first career grand slam on April 20th. In this game, the Angels were playing against the Detroit Tigers. Mike posted his grand slam off Tigers' pitcher Rick Porcello. This capped a 10-run inning for the Angels. This also became the Angels' highest scoring inning of the past 18 years.

Mike did not start his sophomore year as well as his rookie season. According to him, he did struggle early in his sophomore season because he was putting too much pressure on himself and he was chasing pitches that were out of the strike zone.

In May, with Bourjos sidelined once again, the versatile Mike Trout returned to his favorite position, centerfield. In addition to finding his groove on defense, Mike regained the form that made him arguably the most feared hitter in all of baseball during the previous season.

Finally relieved from the pressure of chasing pitches out of the strike zone, Mike recorded a hitting percentage of .327, knocked out 8 home runs, registered 21 RBI, and scored 27 total times.

In this same month, he achieved the rare "cycle", an accomplishment that dictates a player to hit a single, a double, a triple, and a home run within a single game. Only a few hundred players in the history of the game have been able to do so, and Mike was the youngest to ever accomplish the feat in the American League.

By June, Coach Mike Scioscia returned Mike to left field, once Bourjos recovered from his injury. While this did not sit well with some Angels' fans, Scioscia explained that Mike's increase in numbers was more of a result of batting order and subsiding hype, rather than defensive position.

In the same month, Mike was promoted by Scioscia, as the Angels' leadoff hitter, with shortstop Erik Aybar struggling. Mike immediately made an impact, going 3 for 5, with 2 doubles and a stolen base. He also recorded an RBI, base on balls, and 2 runs scored. Mike's all-around game helped the Angels win in the first game of a doubleheader against the Boston Red Sox.

This versatility that Mike displayed on the offensive and defensive side of the ball showed that he is willing to sacrifice his comfortability in favor of doing what is best for the team. As a star player who could begin to get lost in his own hype, it would be understandable if he combatted his coach's decision to shuffle him around the line-up or adjust his position in the outfield.

What separates Mike from some other superstars and what makes him truly great, is that his desire to win is more important to him than what his stat line looks like. As fans of

Mike, we can take this lesson and think about where we let our ego prevent us from doing what is right or best for the collective.

In the same month, Mike scored his 200th run in his 249th game, becoming the fastest player to post 200 runs in more than 70 years. This was made possible when, on June 10th, Bourjos returned to the Angels' lineup. This moved Mike back to left field. This made him the fastest player to achieve this particular feat since Ted Williams and Barney McCosky. Williams set his record in his 225th game while McCosky did in his 236th.

Because of his stellar performance, Mike was named, once again, as an All-Star for the American League team. He was the leading vote-getter among all AL outfielders, and he also finished as the first Angels player to start in the All-Star Game since the legendary Vladimir Guerrero.

Probably motivated by being named as an All-Star starter, Mike continued to build on his impressive sophomore run. In the month of July, not only was he the only player to reach base in every game of the month, but he also registered a .475 on-base percentage and an OPS of 1.108.

Of course, the eye-popping statistics continued in August, when he batted .337 with 6 home runs and a .500 on-base percentage. And while his form somewhat declined later in the season, he was still considered among the most feared and consistent hitters in all of baseball.

By the end of the season, Mike was, once again, in contention for Most Valuable Player honors. His main competition for the award was Miguel Cabrera of the Tigers. By the end of the season, statistics pointed in Mike's favor.

He led the entire league in WAR with 9.2, and his 110 base on balls led the American League.

He also stepped up his game in some statistical fronts, such as his walk rate improving significantly. However, this wasn't enough; he finished second in the MVP voting to Cabrera once again.

Despite missing out on the MVP, the 2013 season was still a wonderful one for Mike. He proved that his incredible rookie performance was no fluke, and he would be the future of not just the Los Angeles Angels, but also of the entire baseball world.

In a slower-paced sport that is trying its best to stay relevant in a fast-paced world and retain young viewers, Mike is the man for this job. He had now arrived as the future and face of baseball.

Chapter 5:

Mike's MVP Season

In February 2014, there were rumors that the Angels would offer Mike a contract extension. News outlets were reporting that the team was considering giving him a 6-year contract worth $150 million. However, it turned out that Mike signed a 1-year contract worth $1 million.

Despite the lower amount, this is the highest figure ever paid to a baseball player who has not yet achieved eligibility for salary arbitration. And then on March 28th, 2014, the Angels announced that they gave Mike a 6-year contract extension worth $144 million.

On the 19th of April, 2014, Mike recorded four consecutive strikeouts, going 0-4 against Detroit Tiger Max Scherzer. This finally earned him the Golden Sombrero, his first after 353 games of play.

The 15th of May of the same year was another memorable day for Mike. In the game against the Tampa Bay Rays, Mike hit a walk-off home run - the first of his career.

On the 15th of July, Mike played in his third All-Star Game, at Target Field in Minnesota. In this game, Mike went 2-for-3, with a triple, 2 RBI, and a double. This earned him game MVP honors, making him the 2nd youngest All-Star Game MVP, following Ken Griffey, Jr. of 1992.

On the 27th of June, according to ESPN.com's Home Run Tracker, Mike hit the 2014 season's longest home run. He knocked the ball a distance of 489 feet to left-center field of Kaufmann Stadium in Kansas City, Missouri.

Mike played 157 games in his 2014 season. He hit .287 with 39 doubles, 36 home runs, and 9 triples. He also totaled 111 RBI, the most in his career, leading the AL in that category. Mike also had 115 scored runs, an MLB-leading statistic. He also recorded 16 stolen bases.

It came as no surprise when Major League Baseball announced the MVP of the league on November 13th, 2014. Mike was hailed as the unanimous AL MVP. This made him the 6th player in MLB history to become the regular season MVP and the MVP of the All-Star Game in the same campaign.

Despite all the accolades and accomplishments, Mike's 2014 season was actually the worst of the next three seasons as a Major League player after his rookie year. Unfortunately, he struck out 184 times - a league high. That certainly put a damper on what otherwise was a truly elite season.

Additionally, his batting average dropped drastically compared to his previous two seasons, and was the lowest since his rookie year. From .399 in 2012 and .323 in 2013, Mike's batting average dropped to below .300 to only .287.

His on-base percentage, or OBP, also fell from .399 and .432 in 2012 and 2013, to .377 during the 2014 campaign. His 16 stolen bases in 2014 was actually a far cry from his previous seasons. He had a high of 49 in 2012 and stole 33 more bases the following season.

In May, Mike suffered a slump during which he only hit .140/.235/.302 and getting only one home run in 51 plate appearances. Aside from whiffing more pitches, Mike also fouled more. His .283 foul strike percentage was also a career high.

Baseball experts cited Mike's troubles with hitting certain areas of the strike zone as the main reason for the decline in his batting average and increase in strikeouts. The upper and inner thirds of the strike zone has always been an issue for Mike throughout his young career.

He had a .211 average with pitches thrown in the upper third of the strike zone. And opposing teams' pitchers picked up on this and tried to capitalize on this weakness.

Some people also cited Mike's increased swinging as one of the factors for his struggles. Mike did say he would be more aggressive and come out swinging in 2014. Simply put, more swings equal more chances to miss.

The thing is, if his so-called "mediocre" season was good enough to earn him the American League MVP, just imagine what more he can accomplish if he truly plays to the best of his ability. As a matter of fact, Mike pinpointed his faults and signified his intentions to improve his game. He worked hard with the team's staff in correcting his tendency to strike out.

While the external breaks didn't go his way in 2012 and 2013, as Mike finished second to Cabrera in the MVP race in both seasons, few doubted that he was deserving of the awards as well. Few also questioned that he was well on his way to becoming one of the greatest baseball players ever to slug it out on the baseball field.

At the tender age of 23, Mike once again led the league in WAR. What's more impressive was that he had already done so thrice in his young career!

Chapter 6:

2015 Season

Mike's great play continued into the 2015 season. On April 17th, he became Major League Baseball's youngest player to reach 100 stolen bases and 100 home runs. He was only 23 years and 253 days old at that time. He even made a tradition out of hitting home runs on his birthdays. He hit home runs on his 21st, 22nd, and 24th birthdays.

On November 10th, Mike made it to the list of finalists considered for the AL MVP. The co-nominees were Lorenzo Cain, outfielder for the Kansas City Royals, and Josh Donaldson, third baseman of the Toronto Blue Jays. Nine days later, Donaldson was announced the new MVP. Mike finished second with 7 first place, 22 second place, and one third place votes for a total of 304 points. Donaldson garnered 385 points after getting 23 first place and 7 second place votes. This marked the third time Mike finished as runner-up in the MVP race in his four seasons playing in the big leagues.

Mike's hard work and perseverance paid off, as he vastly improved his strikeout statistics. From a career and league high 184 strikeouts in 2014, Mike recorded 26 less in 2015, for a total of 158.

It was higher than his strikeout total during his first two years in the league, but it was still a big improvement from what he garnered from his MVP-winning season. Mike also improved his batting average from .287 to .299, while also getting his second highest on-base percentage in his career with .402.

Mike hit a career-high 41 home runs and had 32 doubles and six triples. He also recorded 11 steals and 90 RBI. Mike led the league in slugging percentage (.591, a career high), OPS (.991), OPS+ (176), and WAR (9.4). He also had career highs in walks (92) and total bases (339).

By the end of the season, Mike was named "Best Major League Baseball Player" at the ESPY Awards. He also received his fourth Silver Slugger Award, marking only the second time a player won the award in four consecutive times at the beginning of his career.

The other person to do so was Mike Piazza. The other Mike won 10 Silver Slugger Awards, was named NL Rookie of the Year, and appeared in 12 All-Star Games. Suffice it to say, Trout is in good company.

What's more striking about all these impressive statistics and awards is that Mike accomplished most of them while playing hurt. Mike suffered a wrist injury in July 2015 while attempting a diving catch. This forced him to miss some games and to play the rest of the season hampered by this injury.

In August, he experienced a decline in his play because of the injury. His batting average during that period went down to .218, while also recording a .352 OBP and a .337 slugging percentage. It's a good thing that Mike recorded unbelievable percentages (.316/.413/.643) outside of August.

Imagine how his numbers would have looked like if he didn't get hurt! He probably would have been the unanimous choice for the AL MVP award.

But one must also consider team performance when it comes to awards. The Angels weren't winning the important games, to put things simply. They failed to reach the postseason after staying in contention for most of the regular season.

If the team was winning more games and comfortably on track to reach the postseason, Mike would have less pressure on his shoulders. The added pressure could have played a part in his struggles - especially in regards to strikeouts due to aggressiveness.

Playing under pressure and setting pain aside to play the game you love are just a few of the attributes common among the greatest athletes ever to play their respective sports.

Chapter 7:

The Future

For some observers of the game, Mike Trout could be considered lightning in a bottle; someone nobody expected to make an overnight impact, but he still did. However, for people who have seen him play up close, it is obvious that this guy had it, even from the very beginning.

His father, Jeff, gave him a lot of his physical tools, as a player, and also has been influential in shaping his passion for the game. Also, both Little League and Prep coaches, along with scouts, recognized this guy definitely had the skills to hang with kids much older than him.

After getting drafted, Mike was sent to the Minor Leagues, where he promptly made an impact on each of his stops. And now that he has reached the big leagues, he has taken it by storm as one of the best young players in baseball history.

All of this success, to the casual baseball fan, looks as if it came so quick and easily. But, that surface level view does not truly encapsulate this man. His physical size allows him to have enough strength to hammer balls out of the playing field.

Also, he has amazing speed, something that was recognized even during his prep days. Because of this combination of quickness and power, Mike is considered the second coming of legends such as Kirby Puckett, Rickey Henderson, and even Mickey Mantle.

But other than the athleticism and the sheer skill, some intangibles make Mike tick. Take for example, his patience and instincts. It is this patience that allows him to make all the timely plays on both offense and defense. It allows him to steal bases at an impressive rate and chase down home runs on defense.

For a player who is expected to lead his team on a nightly basis, he is surprisingly patient at the plate for his young age. When he gets in a slump and starts chasing, he is quick to pause, evaluate, and optimize his swing, timing, and presence.

But one thing that makes Mike such a favorite for both teammates and fans is his passion for the game. His love for the game is evident every time he steps onto the field. Teammates, including veterans, vouch for his locker room presence, saying that the excitement he provides, on and off the baseball field, is positive for the team.

That's something any superstar on any team sport should be capable of doing, and Mike is doing it with flying colors. If your best player loves to come to work early and enthusiastically work on his game, imagine the impact that has on everyone else on the roster.

As for his love affair with the fans, don't expect it to end anytime soon. Even though he has only worn the Angels uniform full-time for four years, he is considered a bonafide Angel by even the oldest fans of the team. It is not just that he's unleashed a run for the ages, but his game has resonated with the fan base.

There's a reason he has earned nicknames such as "King Fish 2.0" and "Prince Fish". This early in his career, he is being compared to Angel legend Tim Salmon, and deservedly so.

So, what does the future hold for the one and only Mike Trout? There is no way to actually tell. Given his massive production and still-untapped potential, there's hope that he'll someday be ranked among the best to ever lace them up.

Will he complete his career in Los Angeles? Will he be able to live up to the hype of his first 4 seasons? Only time will tell. However, Mike seems destined for greatness, and it's only a matter of him seizing the opportunity.

Conclusion

Hopefully this book was able to help you gain inspiration from the life of Mike Trout, one of the best players currently playing in Major League Baseball.

The rise and fall of a star is often the cause for much wonder, but most stars have an expiration date. In baseball, once a star player reaches his mid- to late-thirties, it is often time to contemplate retirement. What will be left in people's minds about that fading star?

In Mike's case, people will remember how he came onto the scene for the Angels and helped boost the team's energy. He will be remembered as the guy who had four of the best years ever to start a career.

Mike has also inspired so many people because he is the star who never fails to connect with diehards and make baseball fun to watch for the casual fan. Noted for his ability to impose his will on any game, he is a joy to watch on the baseball field.

At the same time, he is one of the nicest guys outside the field, willing to help teammates and give back to fans. Last but not least, he's remarkable for remaining pure and firm with his principles in spite of his immense popularity.

Hopefully, you've learned some great things about Mike in this book and are able to apply some of the lessons to your own life! Good luck on your journey!

Made in the USA
Coppell, TX
02 December 2019

12255199R00046